Gray Sunshine

Other Books by Leo Zarko

For Children:

Dorothea the Dog Rescuer
Rupert's Happy Home
My First Fish
Safety Squirrel
Farah Wants to Fly
Mory the Mouse
Sidney the Songbird
Wendy the Weed
Cozy & Zeno
Pauley's Piano
Arty the Artist
The Animals And The Mirror
The Visiting Cat
Anxious Annie

Poetry:

Something About Me
Just a Thought
From Me to You
Drifting
Searching

Gray Sunshine

Poetry by Leo Zarko

Illustrations by Gerardo R Madrigal

Gray Sunshine Copyright © 2020 by Leo Zarko

Illustrations and cover design by Gerardo R. Madrigal

ISBN: 979-8-57749-791-0 (soft cover)

All rights reserved. In accordance with the U.S. Copyright Act of 1976, no part of this publication may be reproduced, distributed, or transmitted in any form or by any means, or stored in a database or retrieval system, without prior written permission of the author.

Bringing Joy to Others is a Gift.

Give it Often!

God Bless

Accepting

There was no breakup, I just never saw you again
Still, thoughts of you occasionally make me pick up my pen
The leaves on the trees understand letting go in the fall
It's not the big things I remember, it's usually the small
There's stillness in this house, car keys lying on the table
We couldn't get it right so we never gave it a label
Some of us get lucky living long enough to grow old
A flannel shirt hanging over a chair in case I get cold
Rain drops in a field and the smell of rich black dirt
Memories are powerful, they can bring on the hurt
I won't forget you and the time we spent together
Accepting life also means accepting the weather

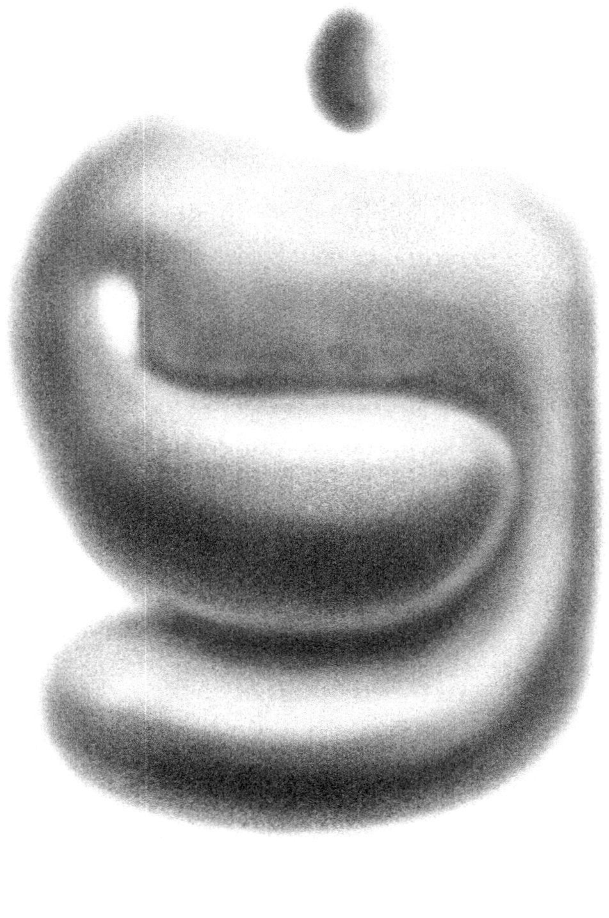

Alcohol-Free

Drinking was very seductive, but it came at such a cost
The bottle gave the wrong directions and I knew I was lost
Happy hour was continual and it seemed to last all day
Whatever the reason, I had no reason for acting that way
I administered self-destruction drop after drop
I frequently told myself I had the power to stop
The boss man warned me about punching in late
I was that outgoing personality that rarely had a date
Checking my hands daily because I often had the shakes
Being robbed of my life because that's what alcohol takes
The sun would rise, but I couldn't get out of bed
The cold showers and the hangover pounding in my head
Dark bar rooms with liquor spilled all over the floor
Falling off a bar stool and stumbling towards the door
I passed roads leading towards help at every junction
Being inebriated made it somewhat difficult to function
Such a waste of precious time I mindfully acknowledge
A million lessons learned and I didn't learn them in college
Blame it on youth and stupidity or just blame it on me
God's intercession finds me years later still alcohol free

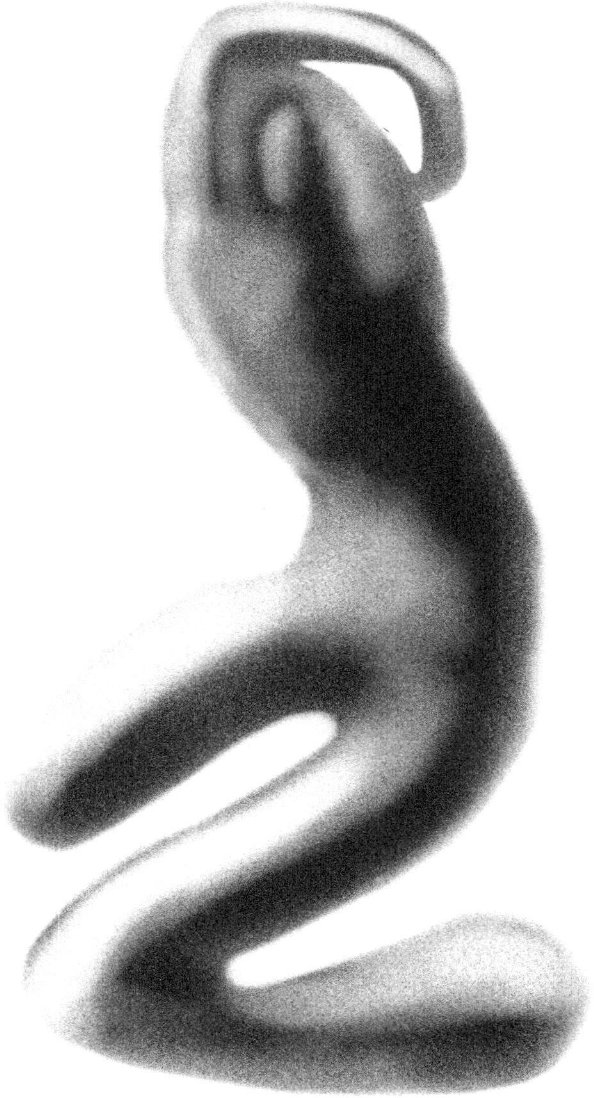

Angels

Once you've met an angel it changes you
They live among us doing what they do
They seek what's right and it doesn't equal power
They're colorful and gentle, remarkable like a flower
Eyes that pierce the soul in a loving kind of way
You can't see their wings, but they wear them each day
Overflowing with compassion their smiles are so true
Such a blessing knowing they've touched me and you
When they're gone that's when we truly value their worth
They return to heaven leaving one less angel here on earth

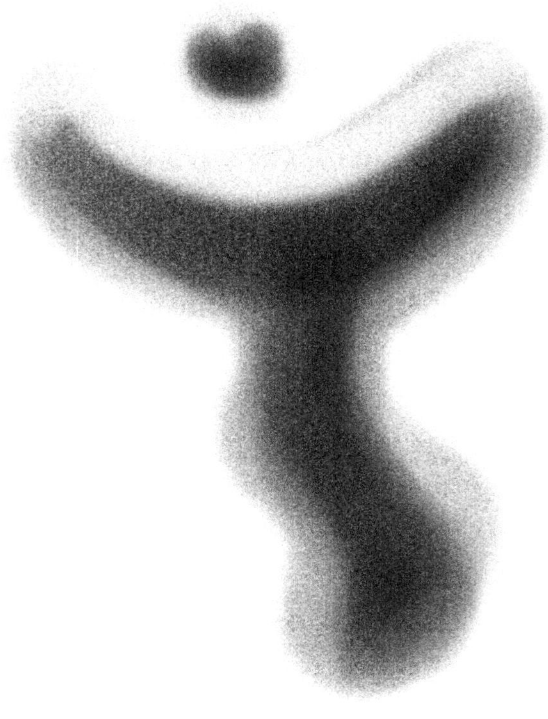

Becoming Someone Else

Emotionally untouchable tougher than them all
Small people don't exists when standing so tall
You pick the time and you dictate the pace
Imaginary finish line like everything's a race
Rusted iron posture with that large stoic resistance
A dominant vibe felt from just about any distance
I perceive you've lost your way and built up a wall
You obviously had to stand before you could crawl
A million bad experiences can make a heart grow cold
Being robbed young can make anyone prematurely old
It's sad you share this deep-seated pain only with yourself
Love and all its potential sitting dormant on a shelf
You abandoned your needs in exchange for self protection
The world is unbearable when you don't feel any affection

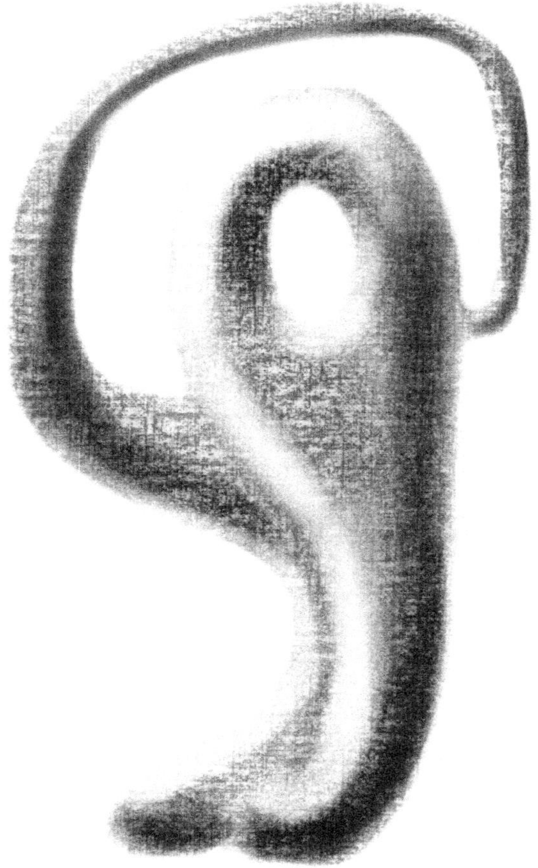

Climbing Uphill

I wanted your love, but truly couldn't handle it
Too many puzzle pieces and some just never fit
Autumn leaves in the yard circling around an old rake
Questioning what's real when everything seems fake
A swimming pool draining as the water keeps leaking
A porch swing with blues music dramatically speaking
Ever so depleted and yet the mind refuses to stand still
Falling downward sometimes feels like climbing uphill

ॐ

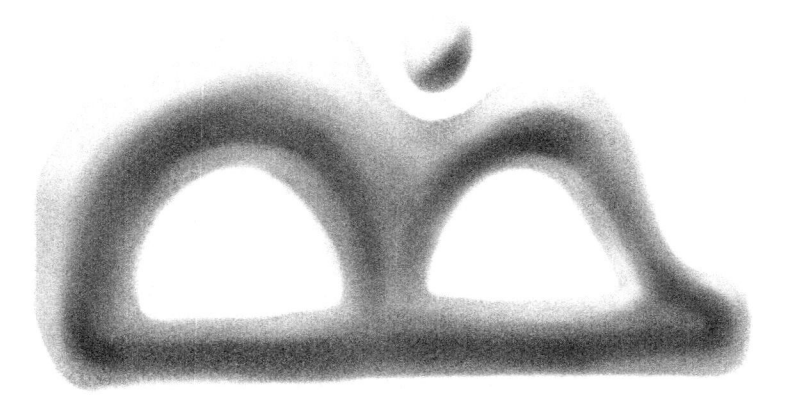

Cologne And Perfume

It's to be expected when hot turns to cold
Some bottles of wine aren't meant to grow old
Lust and longing are selfish and consuming
Good for each other or at least we were assuming
Cuddling has been replaced with other things to do
Sometimes one and one don't add up to two
Using each other maybe perhaps or just a bit
Putting our clothes on, back-to-back we sit
We use to blush afterwards and both say "wow"
The smell of cologne and perfume are only memories now

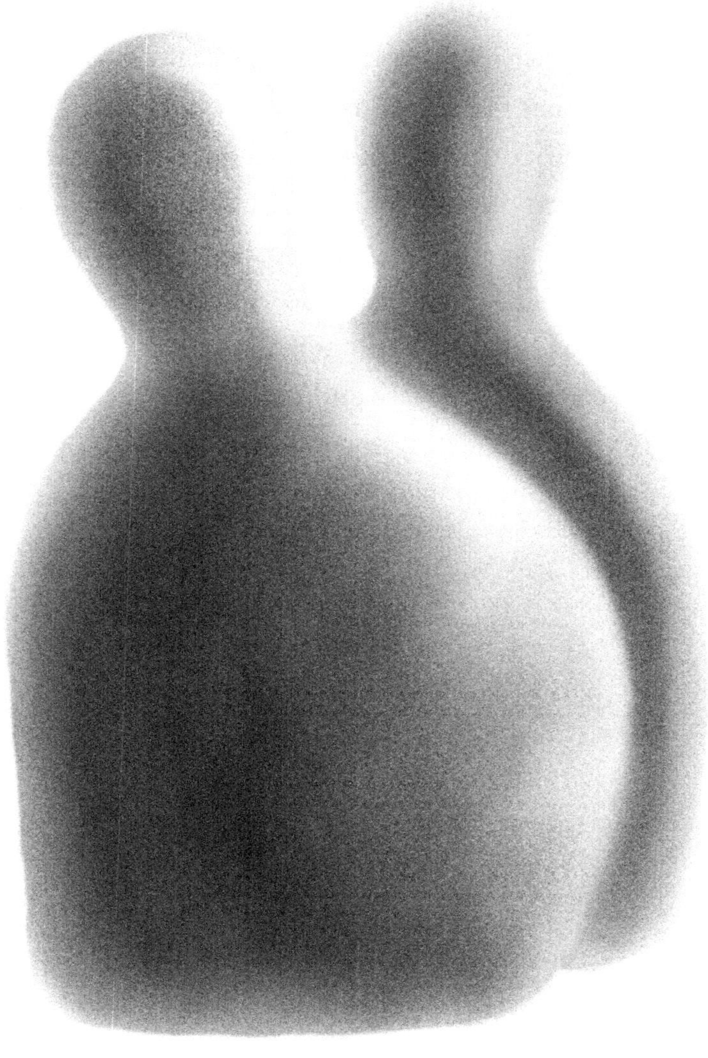

Comparisons

Tall dark and handsome with nice thick hair
Envy accomplishes nothing so why should I care
Honors student with a framed diploma from college
I'm not smart, but I probably have more knowledge
Big house, luxury car, and a picture perfect wife
If I'm focusing on them I'm not really living my life
Mingling with the celebrities and the designer clothes
I don't need to fake it, and I can't do that turned up nose
TV sets, stereos, and that super advanced phone
I'd rather be admiring nature and taking a walk alone
Comparisons are unhealthy and make me feel incomplete
Things that have nothing to do with me I just simply delete

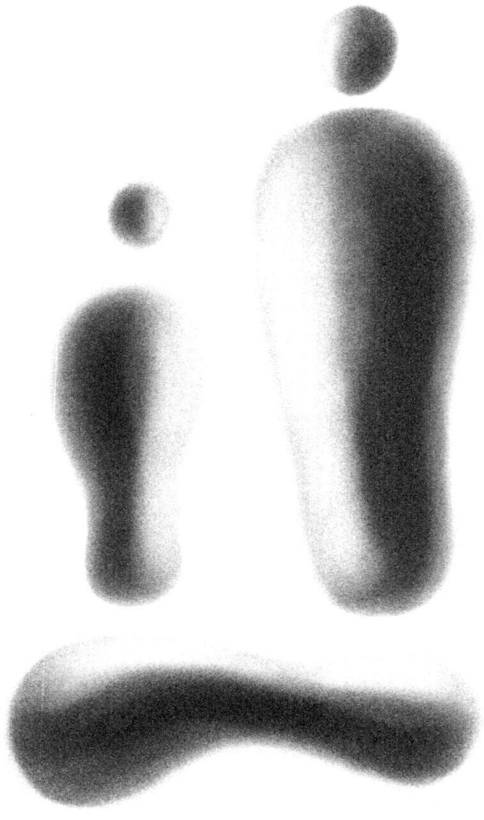

Dashboard Lights

Something orange with blue overtones
Driver seat, flesh, blood and bones
Pavement dark with a single white line
My mind is somewhere else sitting at a stop sign
Windows rolled down I breathe in the fresh air
I wish I didn't worry and I wish I didn't care
The truth is when I drive I feel more in control
Me, my automobile and thoughts for my soul

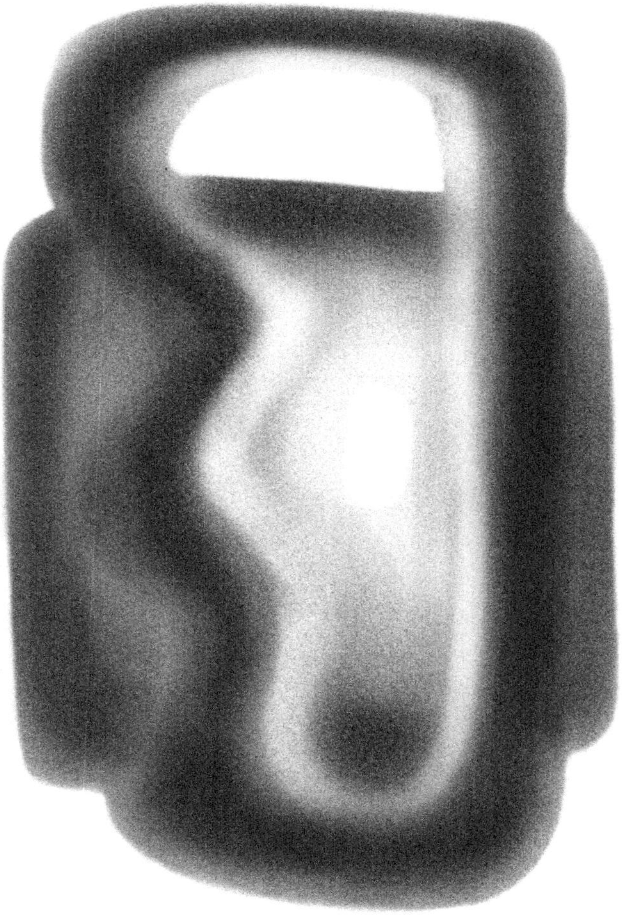

Depressing

People say my writing is depressing and I have to agree
A darkness that never lets the sunshine truly shine free
Head down, arms crossed and a closed bathroom door
A long hot shower and that forever cold floor
Invisible jail cell with no key for that invisible lock
Depression is a bad investment and yet I own stock
No pity for me because I never want to be that guy
I get up every morning and every morning I try

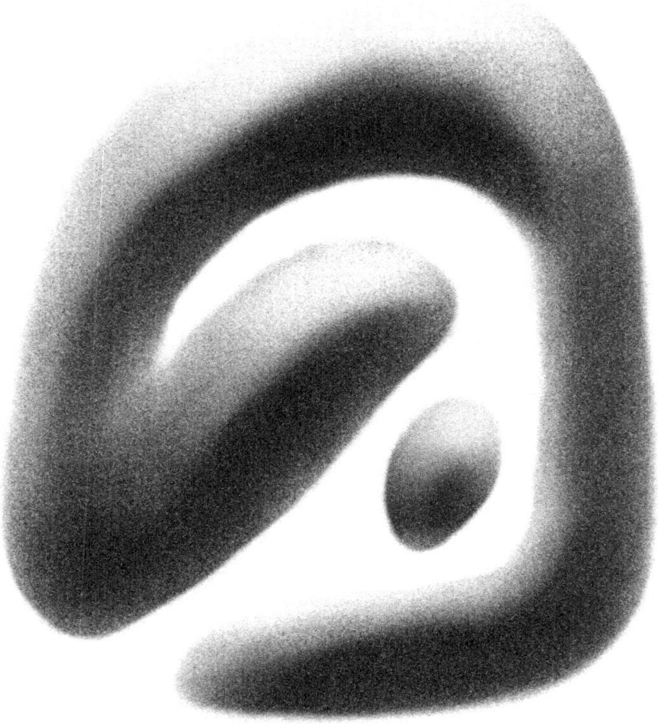

Dive Bar

If you don't want, you don't have to deal with loss
They say a rolling stone will gather no moss
Why stick to a web when you know about the spider
I'd smoke this damn cigarette if I only had a lighter
Staring at whisky bottles even though I don't drink
Elbow on a bar coaster with plenty of time to think
Late dusk sunbeams shine though the tavern door
Addicts hanging out front looking to make a score
Two lovers sit at the end of the bar drowning in booze
This atmosphere feels like a real predictable place to lose
The crowd drinks their troubles away as I ponder why
I know the truth, but I romance it with a lie
Once the sun goes down I'll step out into the night air
I'm not in a hurry because I don't have to be anywhere

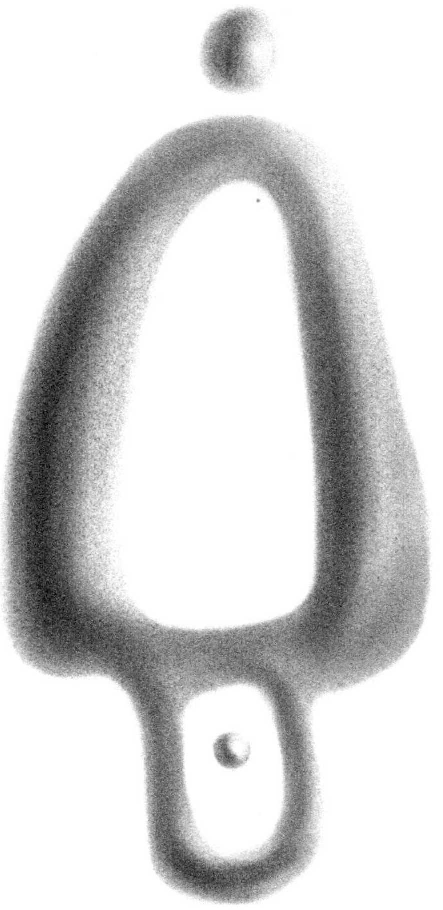

Divorce

It's a state of mind that develops over time
The bad grapes slowly spoiled the fine wine
Kissing with no meaning isn't good for the soul
The acting more complex than any given role
Facial features contorted into an agonizing frown
Remembering love making and hanging around
The silence gets louder and the coldness even colder
No more back rubs and no more kisses on the shoulder
The decision is meant to stop the madness
Despite it all there's a great deal of sadness

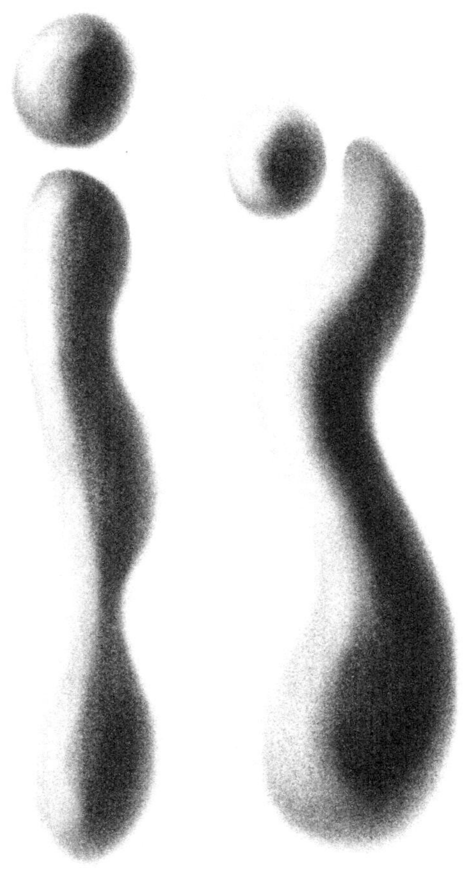

Documentary

So many sweet things akin to so many things gone sour
We're not a documentary summed up in just one hour
Scenic mountain tops and valleys seemingly low
All that learning and yet what do we really know
The truly good things in life don't come at a cost
Trying to find happiness like it somehow got lost
Documentaries only prove life goes by extremely fast
Love should be your life story and how you made it last

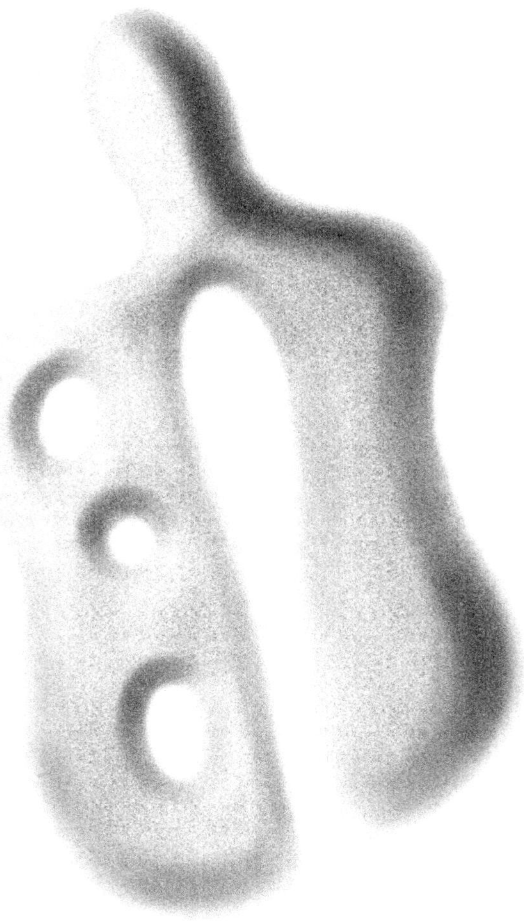

Finding Me

Finding myself at a much later stage
Most of the book is written, but not every page
Sometimes people don't care like I thought they did
I learned early on I was an adult and never a kid
I'm older than my age and it's always been that way
The road has been bumpy, what else can I say
Now I want to be silent and a lot more obscure
Time to heal and time to seek out a cure
Worrying about a world that doesn't worry about me
I have eyes and lately I'm beginning to see
I think there's a difference between what and why
Sometimes I reflect and sometimes I cry
My mood is monotone and yet it's where I should be
Stepping back I find the time to go find me

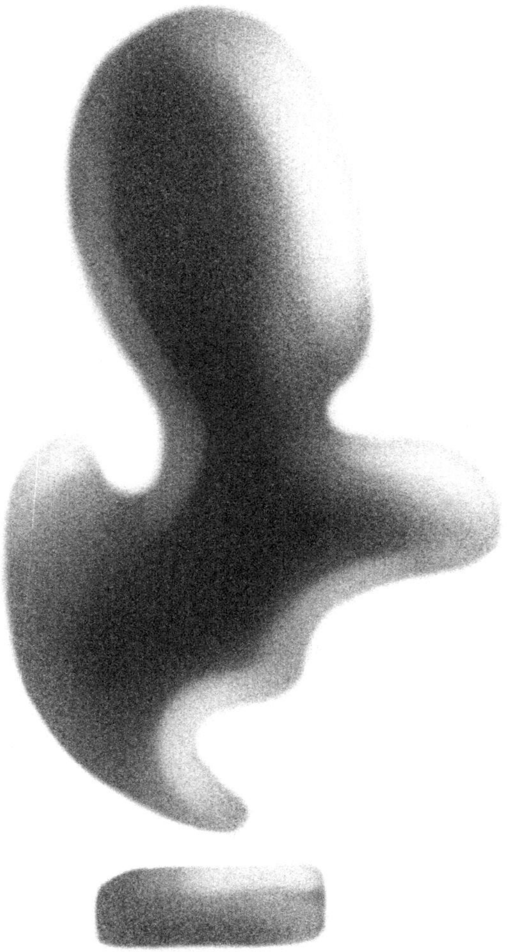

First Dates

She was attractive, but I'm not sure about the rest
I got all dressed up and tried to look my best
The questions were numerous and I honestly replied
She had a host of accomplishments, not sure if she lied
There wasn't any chemistry, no love in the air
I didn't measure up and somehow I didn't care
She ordered a glass for the edge then another for her nerves
No expectations, I've never thought about "deserves"
Working the conversation and I'm losing at chess
I go on these so-called first dates that turn into a mess
The long breaks in between are tough on my self-esteem
Is it just me or does anyone else know what I mean

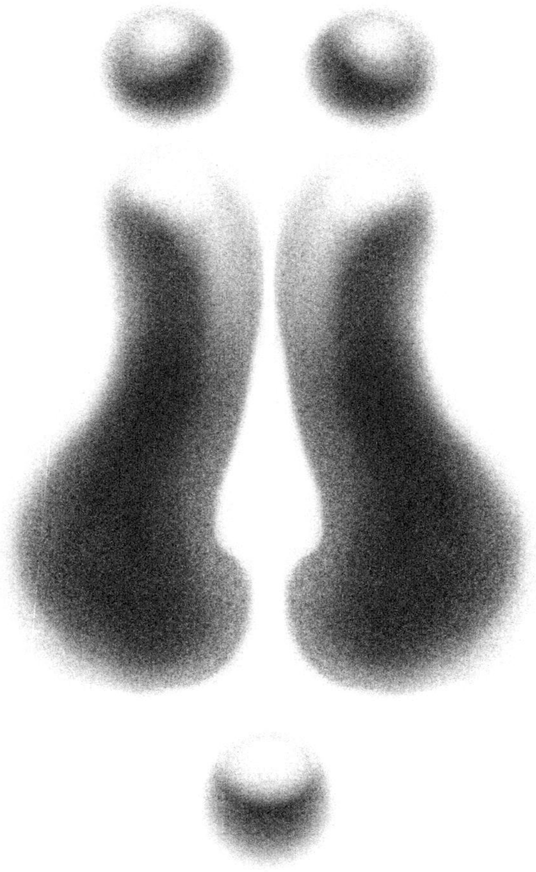

Fresh Air

I could see her whole world in the corner of her eye
A transparent tear clinging as if she could cry
She pulled her hair back and added a little smile
I was staring and I found myself staring for a while
Alone in the crowd she was like artwork on the wall
She was short making all the other women seem tall
Her ring finger was bare, no diamonds or gold
She looked slightly younger or maybe I was slightly old
I could hear her breathing over the music and voices
Like me had she become terribly aware of bad choices
My imagination sometimes leaves me worse for the wear
She walked over and said, "Let's go grab some fresh air"

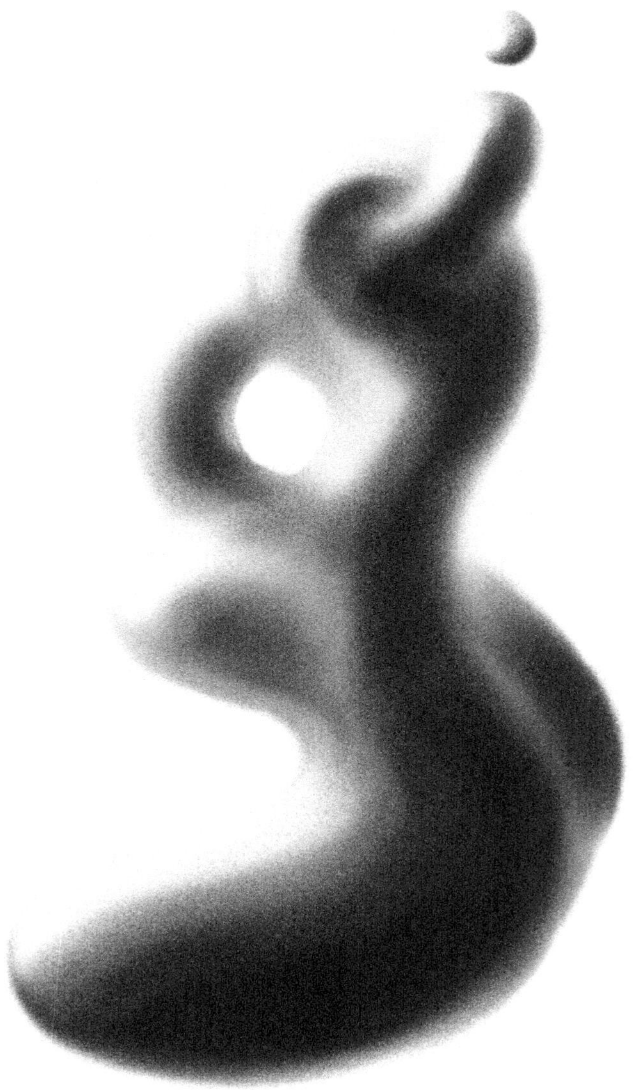

Grab Hold

If you don't miss them you probably didn't care that much
Maybe you took for granted the feel of their touch
The little things were little and yet they are truly missed
Remembering the passion every time you kissed
Fighting just to make up and enjoy the spoils of romance
Smiling from ear to ear after taking a vulnerable chance
Songs you sang together you don't sing anymore
Hearing the doorbell ring and rushing towards the door
Movie night curled up close while lying in bed
Discussing thoughts on the recent book you read
Sitting on the porch talking for hours on end
Reading old love messages, the ones you used to send
You say you didn't love them, but you realized you did
You broke something precious while acting like a kid
Sorry is a consequence and heartbreak is a pain
Love is something you just don't pour down the drain
Memories wrapped neatly and pushed off to the side
Feeling like a kid at the carnival with no money for the ride
Next time you'll love intently before you get too old
When a do-over isn't possible, the past tends to grab hold

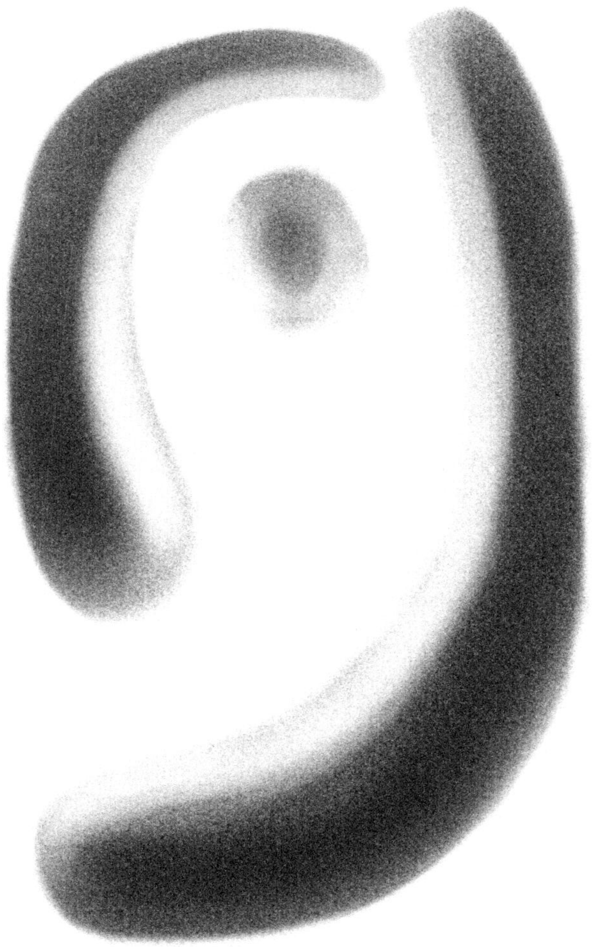

Gray Sunshine

The sun rises at six and yet I choose to sleep in
The clouds have made it gray so today the clouds win
Shades of reality vary depending on my emotional state
I should gather myself up, but I've decided I better wait
Trapped in deep thought ruminating over all that I fear
A million miles away when I couldn't be more near
At night I feel the day that's pushed me hurriedly along
The things I did right and all the things I've done wrong
Car keys in hand and yet no reason to turn the ignition
Gray is persuasive, it contributed to my condition
Gray sunshine is the best I can do so I won't apologize
I'm unqualified to judge and haven't a voice to criticize
Pondering why I've turned into such a melancholy me
Thinking about exit signs when I should just let it all be
Getting a lot of thinking done sitting on a porch stair
Breathing in humidity I feel the heaviness in the air
We all get a bit quieter falling on fewer words to say
Extremely attached in a strange detached kind of way

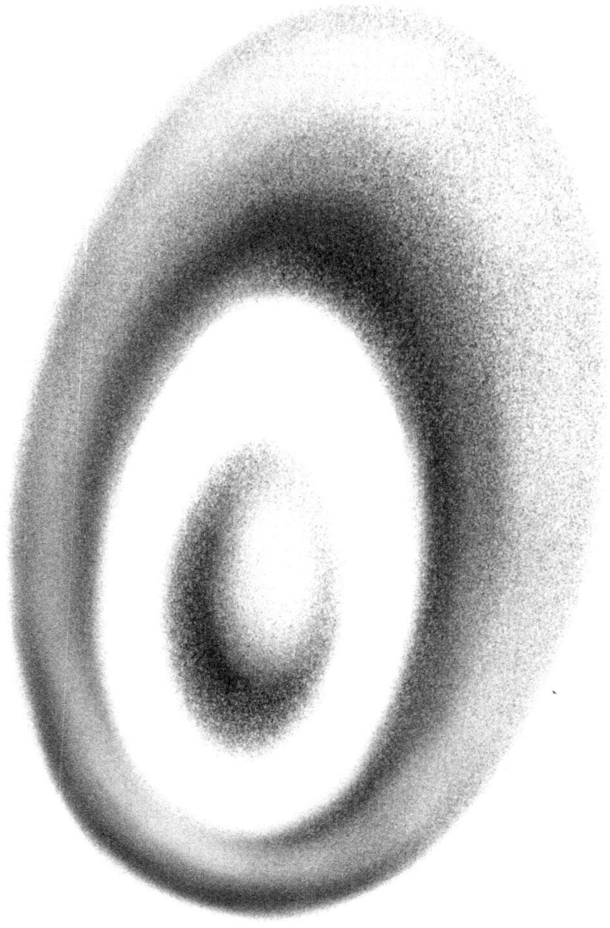

Hazel Eyes

A fabricated idea or wishful thinking
Sometimes floating, sometimes sinking
Rain danced in puddles bringing a close to the day
I didn't know her, but she smiled staring my way
I recall pink lipstick and sandy brown hair
Her eyes were hazel and her skin ever so fair
I wonder if she's a poet and if she'd ever write about me
Maybe, but right now I'm taking in all that I can see
I suddenly like you, and I noticed you like me too
What a nice thing to happen so what should we do
Will my poem be remembered long after reading
My subconscious is kicking in and my mind is conceding
My imagination has feelings even if it's only in my head
Sometimes what you long for reminds you right before bed

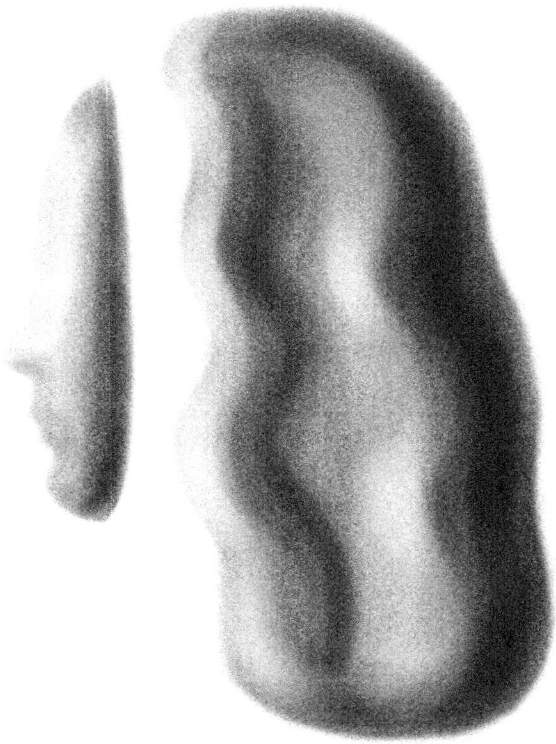

I Love You, Honey

You smile with a frown and your eyes are dim not bright
Something's wrong even though you say it's alright
Drinking straight from the bottle your lips stained red
Resting on a cushion a makeshift prop for your head
A book you haven't finished cries out to you for attention
You look relaxed while displaying a great deal of tension
The television is on with the volume level turned off
One more cigarette to help you with that cough
The rain hits the roof while the clouds fill the sky
I don't bother you, I don't ask you why
When I pass by you I'll run my fingers through your hair
I love you, honey, and I will always profoundly care

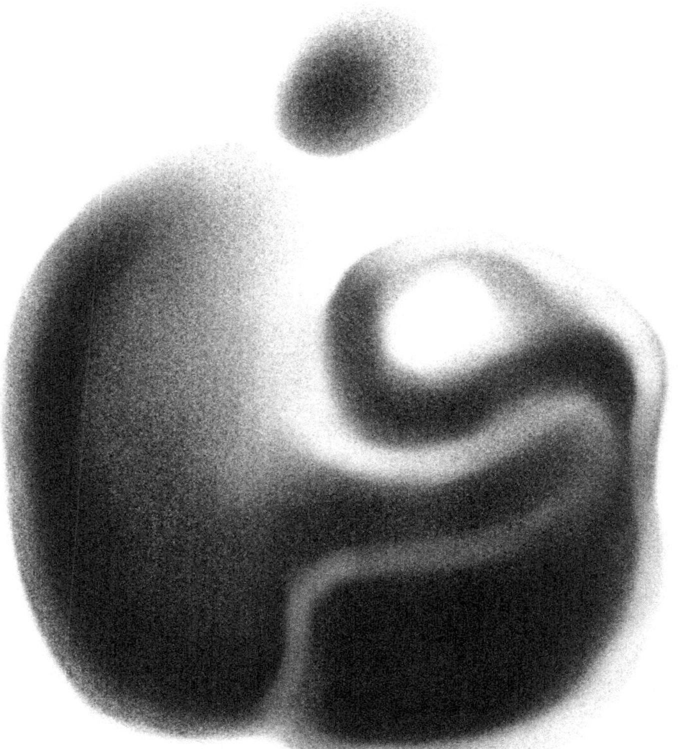

I Write

I write late at night when my heart is open to talk
I write when I see people holding hands on a walk
Sometimes it's a song or a deep hidden emotion
Sometimes I write hypothetically based on a notion
The beautiful world is something I simply can't ignore
The church bells ringing and the angles above the door
Lost friends who have crossed over to the other side
Awe over God's abundant love reaching so wide
Love and hurt coexisting in so many parts of me
Love enthusiastically happy, heartfelt, and free
Sharing openly is part of my true vulnerability
Sharing the spirit of it all with a great deal of humility

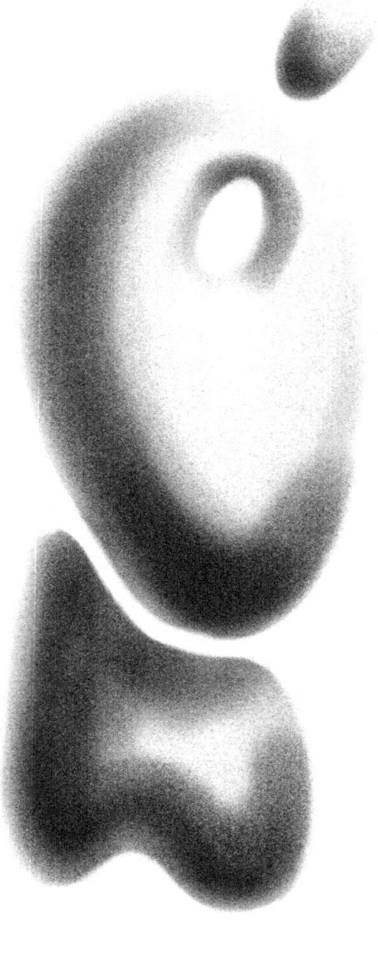

Levee

Stepping back to move beyond who I used to be
I'm determined to find the new and improved me
Change is hard and it doesn't happen overnight
Thought patterns don't just give up without a fight
A complicated life has become something not needed
I've been walking in a garden that really needs to be weeded
Stress builds into depression and that gets quite heavy
When a spillway is needed they usually build a levee

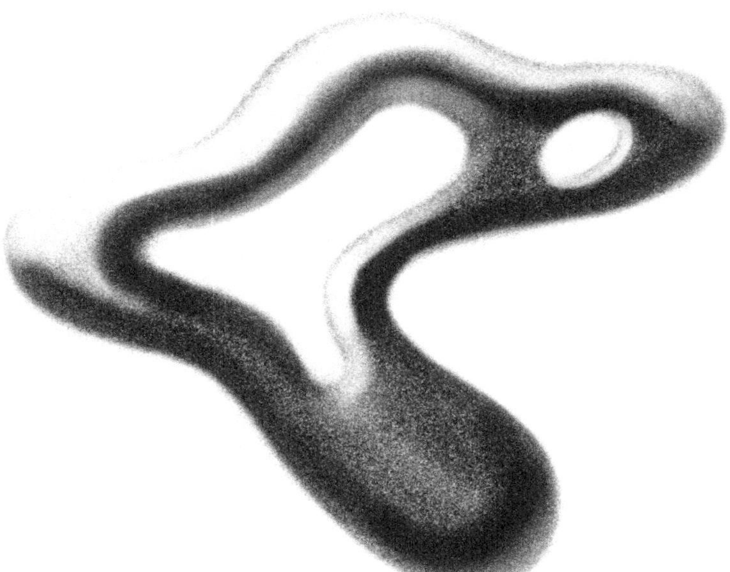

Limits

Getting close means rolling the dice
Being yours actually sounds kind of nice
I feel the heat, but I think it will eventually burn
A little hesitation and a whole lot of concern
The lingering idea of all that togetherness pleasure
Getting and giving abundantly way beyond measure
My feelings always show up in my facial expression
I'd rather progress slowly noting each valuable lesson
Avoiding a relationship doesn't take a lot of acting
I get standoffish when things become way too impacting
When I get too close I automatically envision that line
Vulnerability has limits and lately I've really set mine

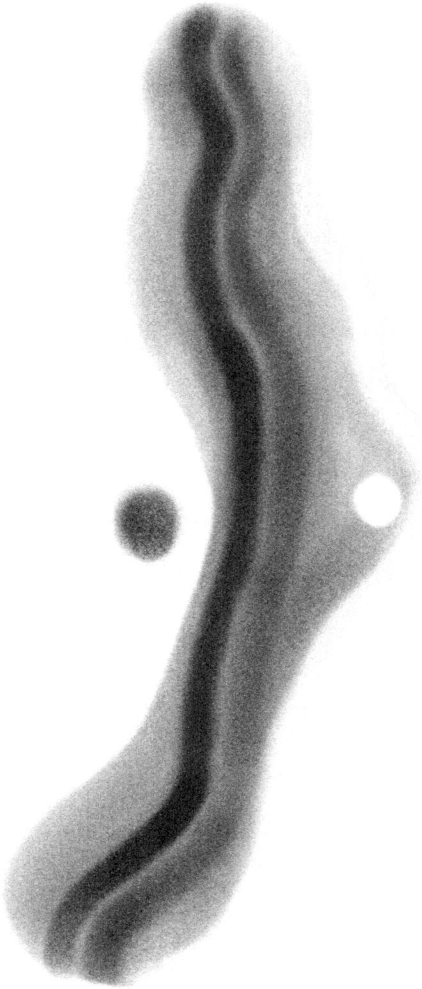

Long Stares

Looking at something or someone not seeing a thing
A song I heard a million times that I don't care to sing
Ocean waves roll over my feet and I don't feel the wet
Why do I gamble knowing full well I won't win the bet
The pains of my body grow with the coming of age
What does it really matter what I write down on this page
I'm numb turning from one thing to another
That lost child who never knew the arms of a mother
I realize I don't understand and rarely have I ever
Life holds promise and yet for me it is a difficult endeavor
Burning late night oil makes the day come along too soon
Falling asleep in the morning and waking around noon
I'm not funny anymore and it definitely effects me inside
I wanted to be the conductor now I'm just along for the ride

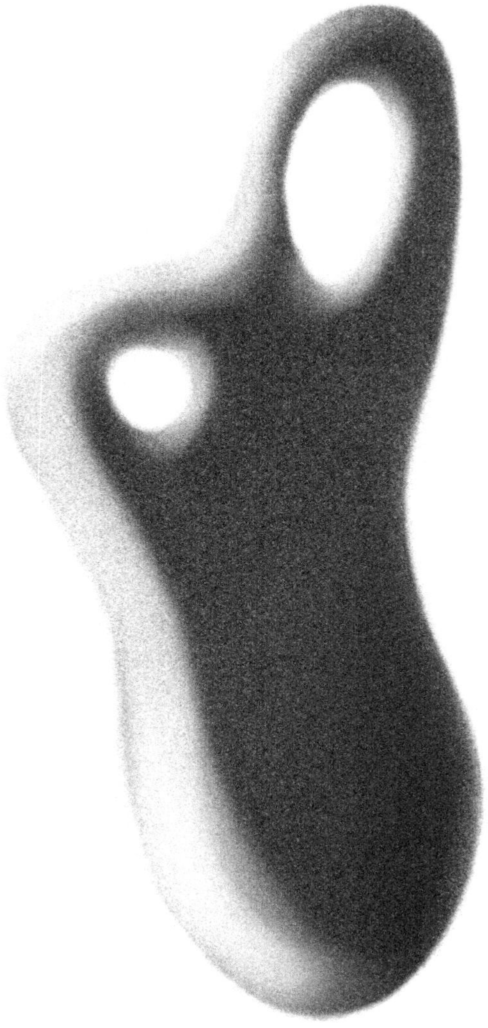

Number One Goal

Gaze in wide wonder the stars of the evening sky
Cry yourself a river if you feel the need to cry
Sing even if you're not crazy about your voice
Kiss like you mean it, it's a far better choice
Expensive possessions cost way more than money
Enjoy the rain drops because life isn't always sunny
Laugh and smile, it happens to be good for your soul
Live a loving life and make that your number one goal

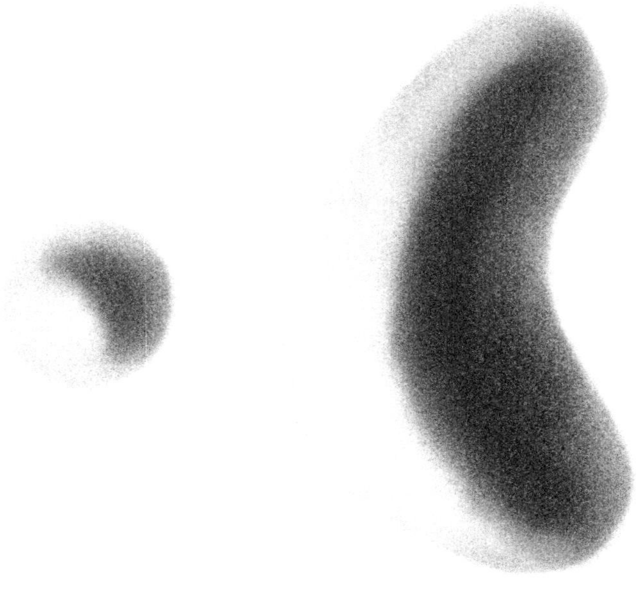

Old House

A noisy furnace kicks on way more than it should
I can't afford to fix things and not sure I would
Single pane windows whistle all hours of the night
The dining room leans downhill and a little to the right
The gravel driveway looks like an old farm house lane
Flagstone basement lit by a light bulb with a chain
The kitchen door squeaks for some unknown reason
Without gutters the icicles hang in the winter season
The walls talk at night and get louder when ignored
Antiques in the attic where things like that are stored
The cement garage floor cracked right down the middle
I grew up like this and it reminds of when I was little

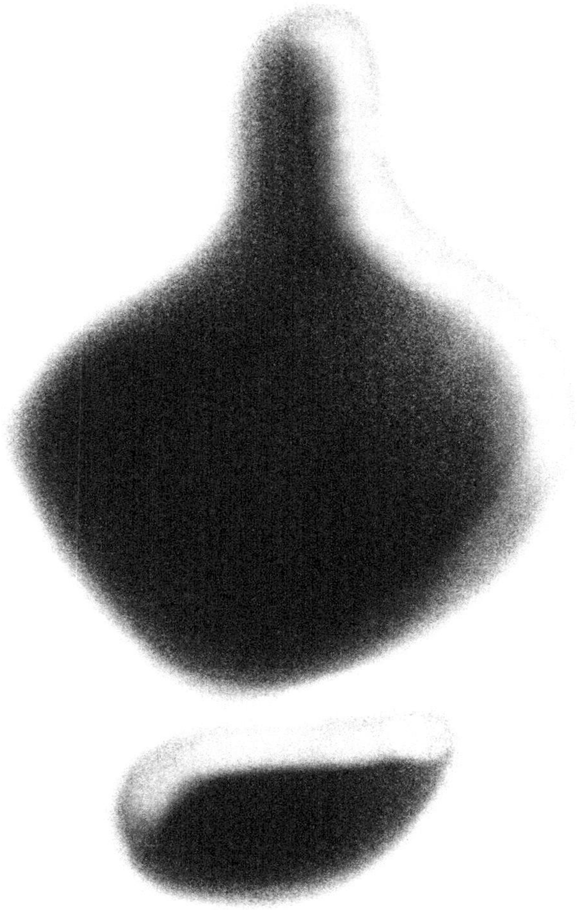

Only A Sip

You're not clay and they're not the potter's hands
Your life is yours regardless of their plans
If you bend they might ask you to break
You like to give and they like to take
Some days they need you, but they set limits on that
One day you're their kitten the next day you're their rat
Sad changing for them when they never change for you
A relationship of one has never added up to two
They guzzle the wine leaving you only a sip
Being a good waiter doesn't guarantee a good tip

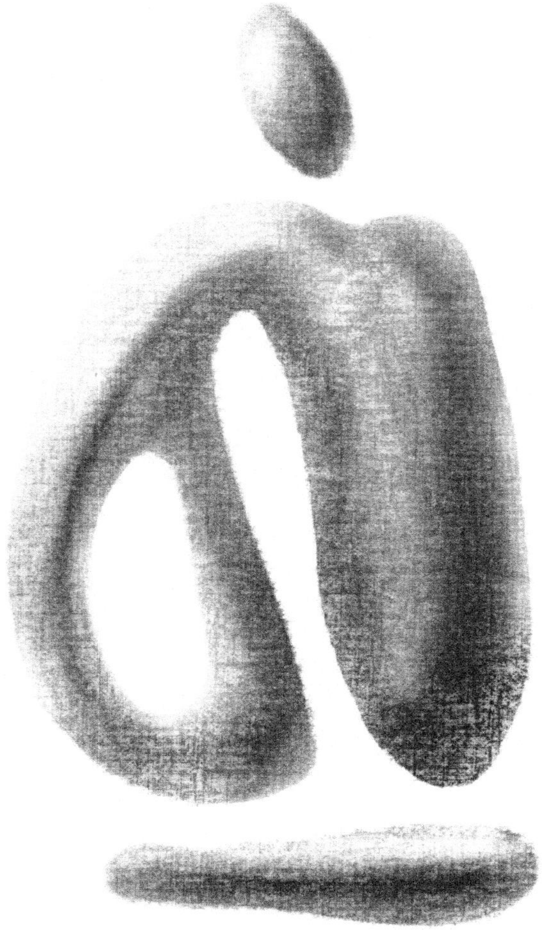

Out For A Walk

Conscious of my smallness I see the world rather large
God is all around me, and He's definitely in charge
I admire nature's artwork and all that colorful detail
The air is calming and feels good when I inhale
Pea gravel sticks to the underside of my boots
Old cottonwoods loom tall with gray brown roots
Birds of the sky descend and congregate together
Sunshine is great, but I like the inclement weather
A fisherman casts his line and lights up a cigarette
I could ruin this moment with shortcomings and regret
Letting go for the moment and truly enjoying the walk
In this environment I listen and find no need to talk

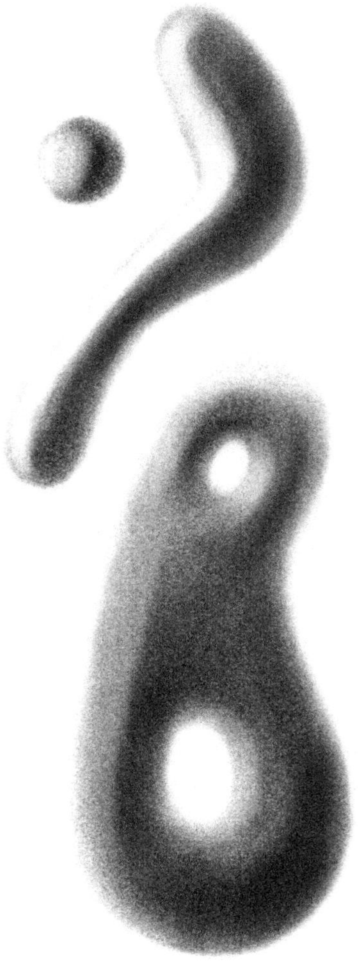

Pinch My Nose

A roll down window and a torn car seat
The sun is hot and I can really feel the heat
Parked by a lake people give a look as I blank stare
I know they have their own lives so why should they care
I'm supposed to meditate, but my mind isn't there
I'm so focused I can see tiny particles in the air
The clock doesn't move and neither do I
The meaning of life and all those questions why
I rest my forehead on the wheel looking at the floorboard
Fifty-eight years in my body, where is everything stored
Old girlfriends and youth gone seemingly way too fast
Have I learned anything or has time just flown past
A look in the mirror and I'm clearly showing my age
Journaling non-stop trying to add substance to each page
Time to start the car because the park is going to close
When those tears start falling I usually pinch my nose

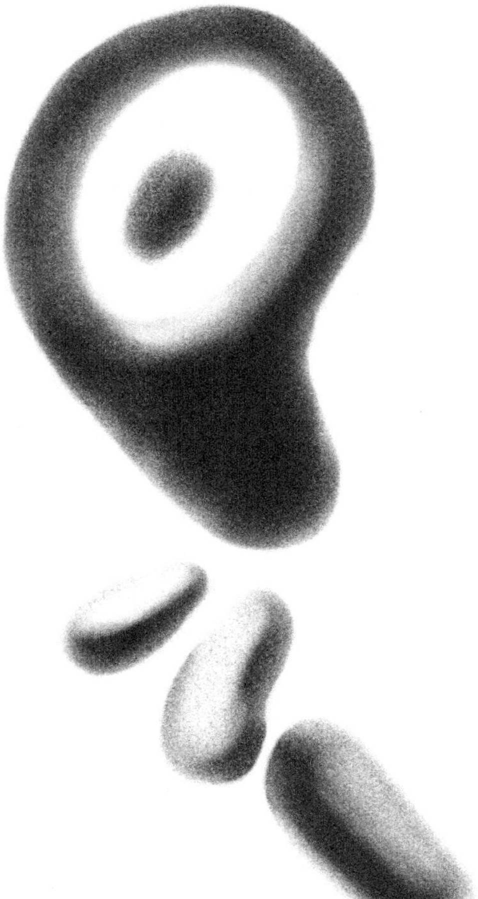

Pink Ribbons

When I heard you had cancer I didn't know what to say
My heart stopped and my thoughts raced every which way
Somehow things seem out of focus and not really clear
I can see you're afraid as you step forward into your fear
Tests and x-rays make it dream like and somehow unreal
One can never be prepared to handle this side of the deal
A million questions about something we know little about
God hears prayers and we believe that way beyond a doubt
The world keeps spinning, but sometimes it just stands still
Reality is never more real especially when one becomes ill
We know about this season and we're all deeply affected
Those pink ribbons mean a lot more than I ever expected

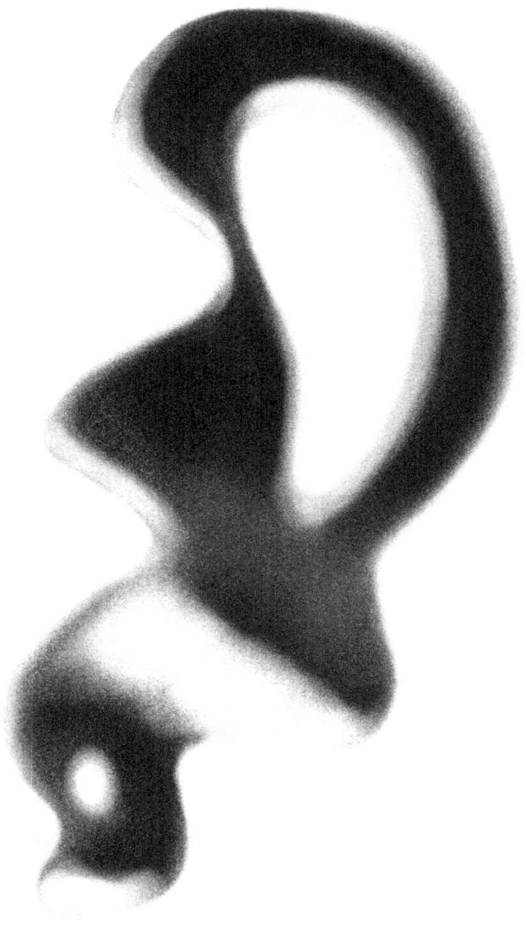

Pretty Face

My heart is intact despite the jagged edges
Things that divide and things that form wedges
Come to me with something more than "just friends"
Don't become wishy-washy or say it all depends
I could love you with all the power of the rising sun
Good things are impossible when one decides to run
Despite the fear love should be genuine and giving
Love feels good and makes life really worth living
One more try hoping things will naturally fall into place
I find nothing better than a smile on a pretty face

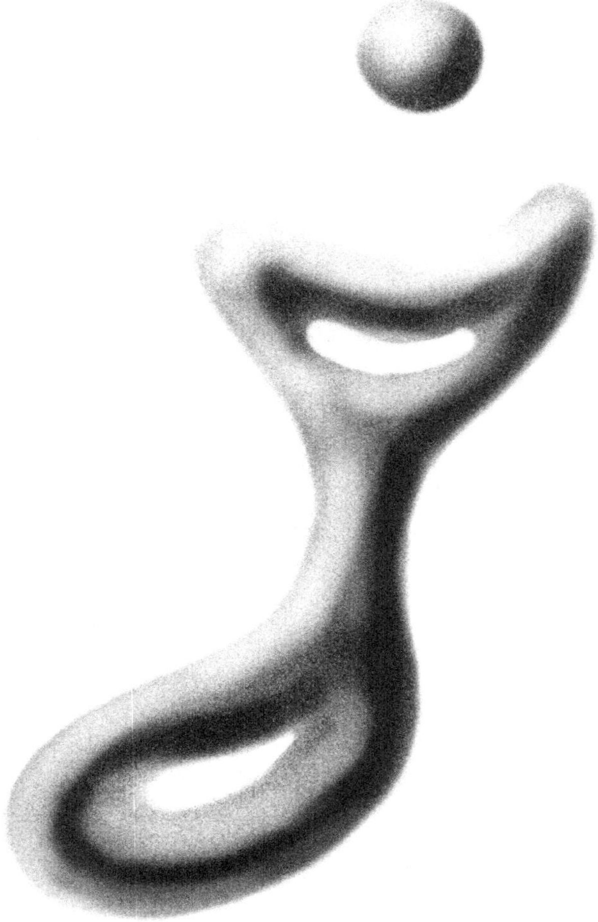

Prove It

Show me you want me because I won't chase you
I fall easily and that's something I don't want to do
Kiss me first and make sure the passion is truly there
Call me for no reason and show me that you care
Squeeze my hand gently and make me feel secure
Give only willingly something loving and pure
Cling to me and don't push away my protection
Hug me tightly and shower me with affection
Speak clearly with your eyes, no words needed
Pick me up when I'm feeling down and defeated
If you're slightly jealous I won't think it's wrong
Find a nice piece of music and we'll call it our song
Sit on my lap in a place where we simply don't fit
I'm ready to love you and I can't wait to prove it

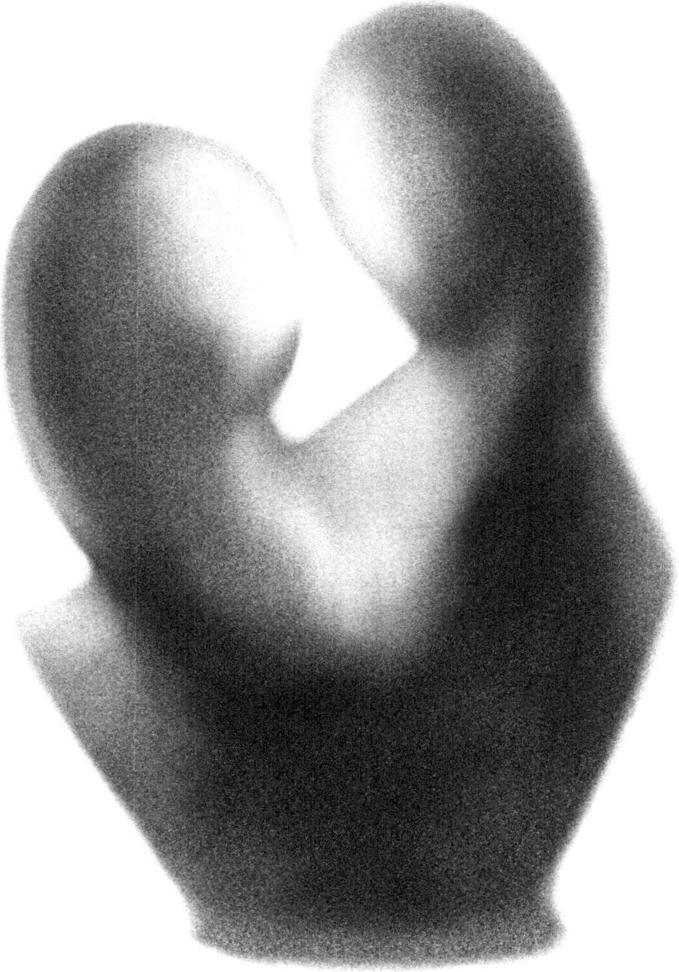

Radio Tower

My mind whispers loudly in the early morning hour
Flashing beacons dance atop that distant radio tower
Car headlights trace as I listen to passing trains
Counting my breaths to slow the blood in my veins
Directing my dreams even before falling asleep
No puffy clouds in the sky and no little white sheep
Ink on my fingers, but I'm too lazy to care
With the windows open I can smell the morning air
There's no companion to greet and no loving embrace
The second hand works precisely at a furious pace
Always uncomfortable I try to lie perfectly still
Will today go easy, or will it seemingly be all up hill
The sky is yet dark and I can see one last star
I count my blessing having made it thus this far

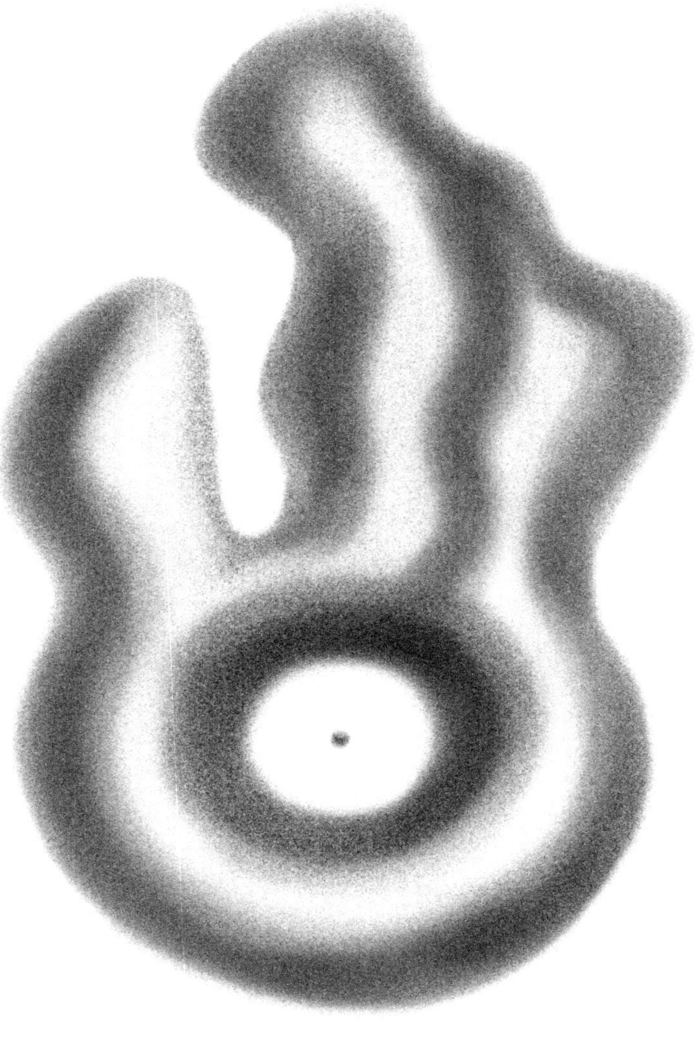

Refuses To See

I used to be exciting and one heck of a flirt
Laughing and joking shrugging off the hurt
Liquid courage really delivered fuel to the fire
When you feel good you just want to get higher
Candle wax disfigured with no trace of the wick
Functioning beyond my ability made me quite sick
Blues bars with strong alcohol flowing like streams
When you pass out you can't remember your dreams
I let something powerful have power over me
Vision is rendered useless when one refuses to see

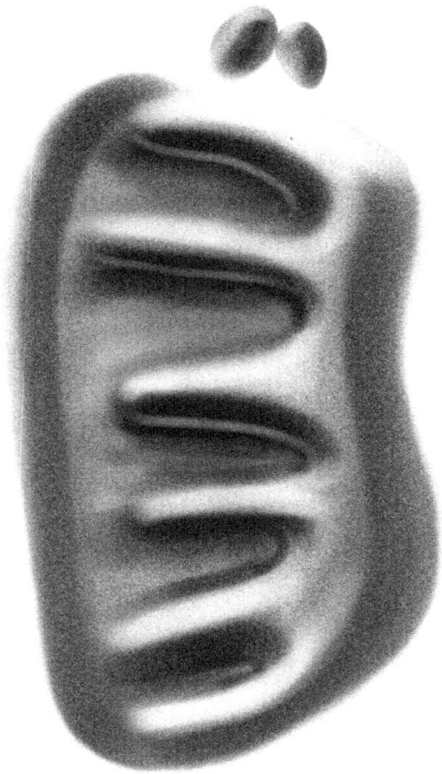

Remembering

A generation aging kind of stuck in their ways
A time referred to as "the good old days"
Calloused hands the so called trademark of a man
The day to day routine with no foreseeable plan
Simple evenings, suppertime then a television show
The moon was bigger and had a better glow
Friday night when the weekly paycheck got spent
A beat up old car, bad tires, and a big ol dent
Education and something about the golden rule
Kids fighting constantly and having trouble in school
Attention not so much, but maybe there was love
The sky just seemed bluer with a heaven up above

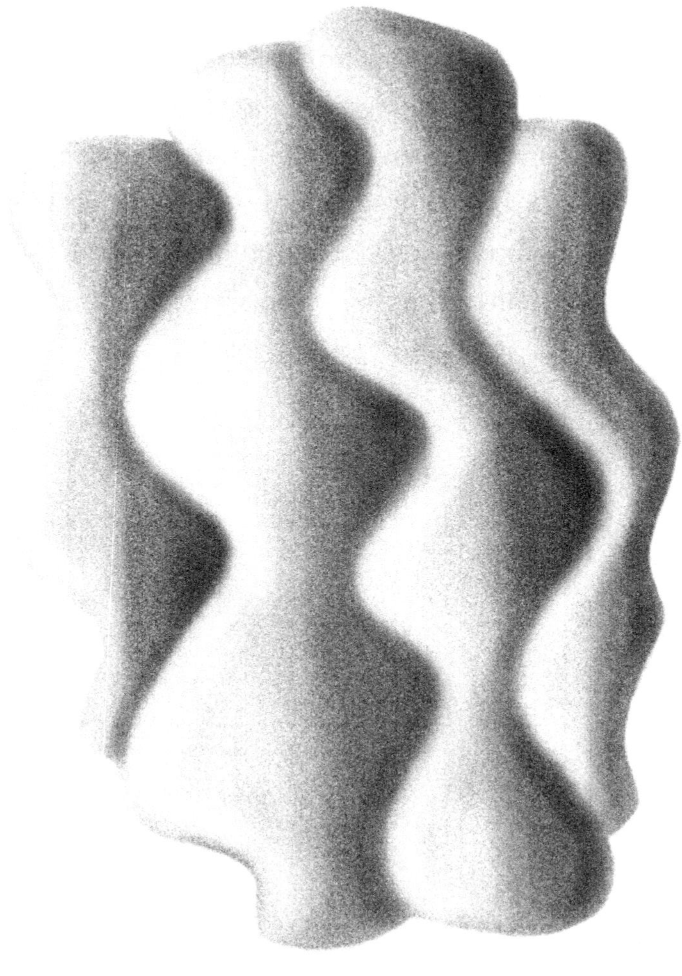

Seeds

My pen is full of ink, but reluctant to write
Meaningless words in a room with dim light
Poems should say something far beyond rhyme
Writer's block like a clock giving up on time
Thoughts, dreams, and a love that last forever
I'm not very smart, but I try my hardest to be clever
Sensitive words must be picked not pulled like weeds
My mind needs cultivating, sunshine, water, and seeds

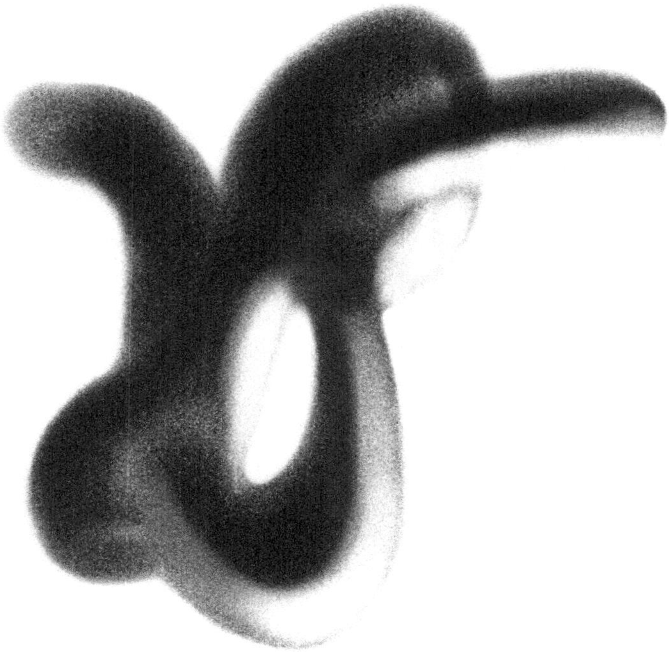

Sleep

No light switch will turn off that endless chatter
Too many thoughts about things that don't even matter
Worries aren't welcome, but they still come around
The darkness certainly has a very distinct sound
The alarm clock is ready with its little red light
Training for the morning like a fighter for a fight
Control over what when it all falls apart
Depression and anxiety like oil paint on art
Prayers are offered up in hopes of a better tomorrow
An unconscious tear for that very conscious sorrow

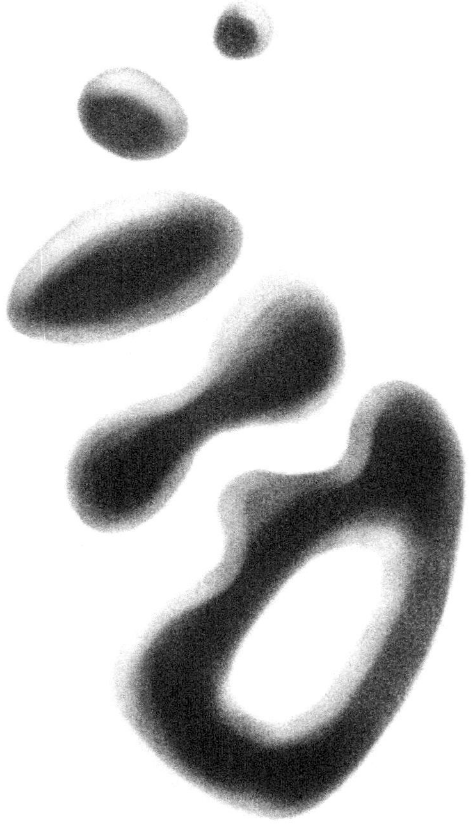

Smoking Cigarettes

Train in the distance with steel wearing out the rail
High school diploma hangs crooked on one tiny nail
Speaking with silence is sometimes the better way
Accumulating ashes and using the floor for an ashtray
Perfect smoke rings take practice and quite a bit of time
Empty pockets and scrounging around for a dime
Regular or menthol like it's some kind of gasoline
That new car smell now smells like tar and nicotine
An acoustic guitar that hasn't been played in awhile
Sitting on a picnic table staring down a country mile
Butane lighter smell and the click of the chrome top
Some smoke a little and some smoke a lot

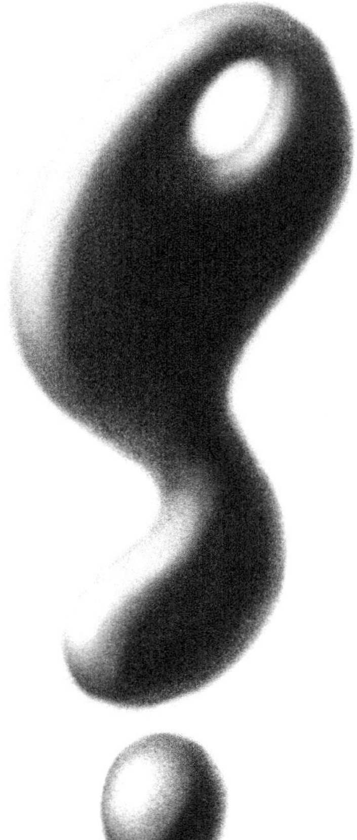

Something Powerful

One note from a blues guitar
A fast engine in a real cool car
Kissing a beautiful woman while holding her tight
Delicious food prepared and cooked just right
Good news from a doctor after a scare
The prettiest girl in the classroom smiles with a stare
A baby's first cry and the joy that it brings
Rain on a tin roof as a little bird sings
An elderly person telling a story from their past
Summer days especially the ones that last
Gospel music causing you to shed a few tears
Flying in an airplane letting go of all your fears
Love and only love truly pure in all its forms
God's divine protection though life's inevitable storms

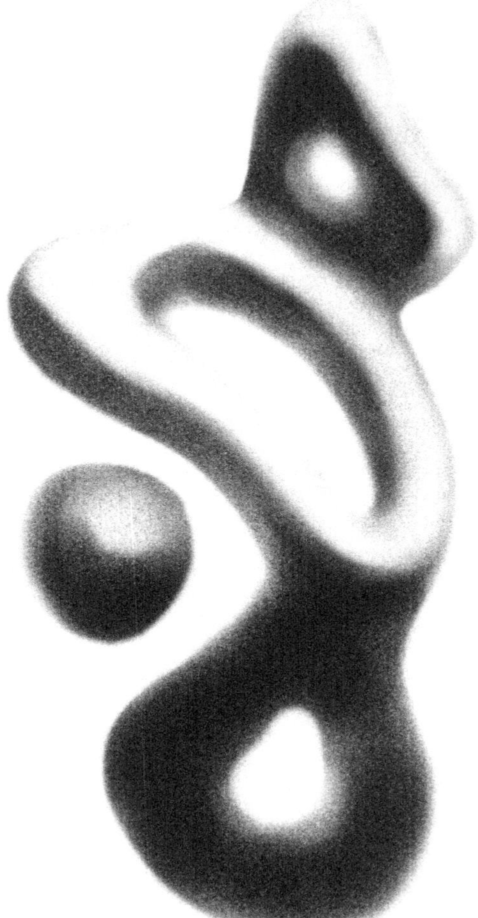

Supporting Actor

Frequently it's the supporting actor who can really act
Life wasn't meant to be easy and that's a realistic fact
Maybe in conclusion there can only be so much changing
Trying so hard to fix life with all that non-stop rearranging
People pleasing can leave one cold and empty inside
Seclusion is a fancy way of saying, "I just want to hide"
Sick of talking and hearing one's own voice
Happy or sad it comes down to a conscious choice
Smile outwardly and be very gentle with that inner sorrow
What's uncomfortable today may be comforting tomorrow
Ruminating over lost time has never rewritten history
The past is unchangeable and the future is a mystery

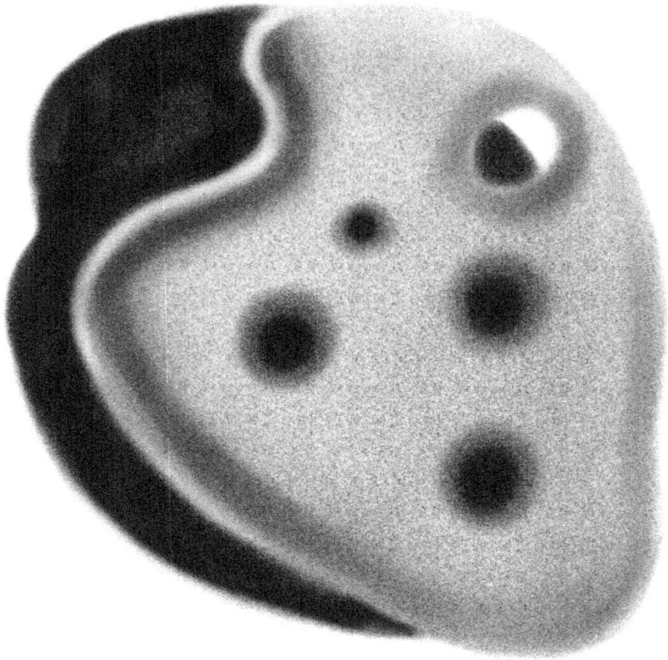

Surface

Way too deep and too heavy for most
Over-serving the guest while trying to be a good host
Striving to find meaning in meaningless things
Pushing a pen at four in the morning as a little bird sings
Viewing things like a puzzle and figuring out where they fit
Never listening to music others may consider a hit
Staring at life and falling in deeper than you should
You thought about the surface, but not sure you could
Your attention span is vast and conversations have to end
You might be too much even for your best friend
Some think like you, but mostly not
The surface seems cold and you prefer it hot
Some of the biggest hurdles stem from you being too deep
Sometimes just being you makes it difficult to sleep
Emotions are useful so don't fret if that's who you are
Keep shining brightly because the universe needs your star

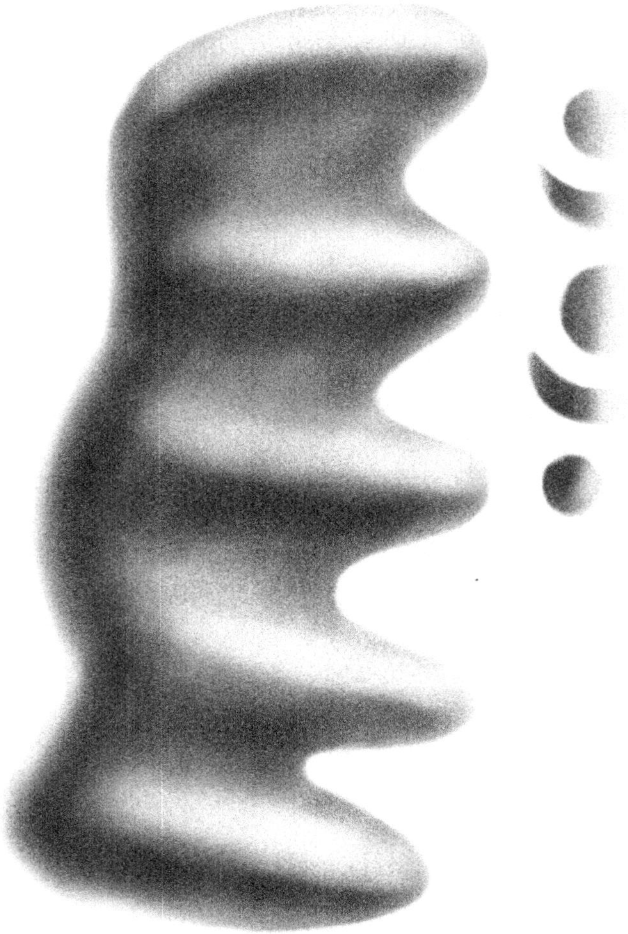

That Way

Like a long winter that never seems to let up
Coffee gone bad staining the inside of my coffee cup
Rocking back and forth running pens out of ink
Forever in a day with plenty of time to think
Out walking I noticed two lovers caught up in romance
Listening to great music I wait on my turn to dance
Happiness comes from loving, not from collecting toys
Quiet isn't relaxing when one craves a little noise
Hearing "I want you" would be such a wonderful sound
One passionate kiss could turn this whole thing around
Love comes and goes, but I certainly wish it would stay
We could love each other and we could keep it that way

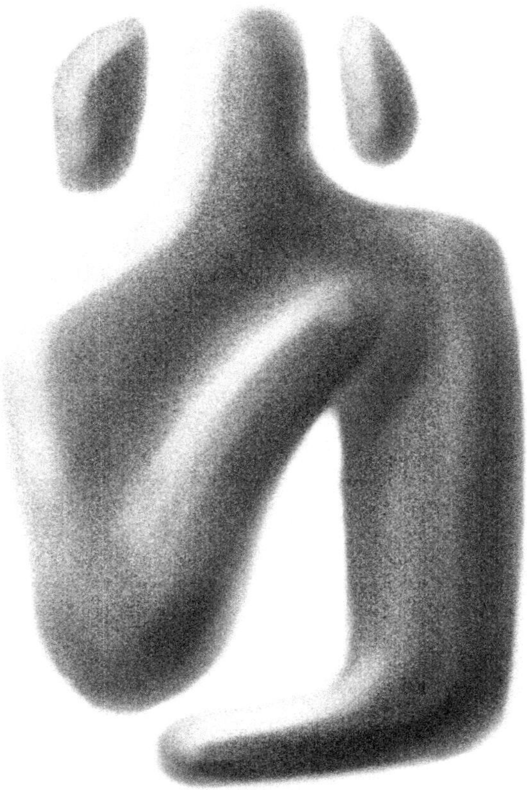

There Comes A Time

We soon realize love should be spread throughout each day
Say kind thoughtful things and act accordingly to that way
Listen intently while showing interest and concern
Learn everything because there's always room to learn
Answer the call when it would be much easier to ignore
Make peace with yourself to stop your own personal war
Return to Mother Nature the love she's constantly giving
Help a poor person get ahead so they can carve out a living
Visit the sick and bring a little sunshine into their day
Thank God daily and make strides to follow in His way
Seek out a meaningful life and a good life you'll find
Go easy on the stress and don't overtax your mind
There comes a time when age hands you a report card
Plant good seeds and you'll end up with a beautiful yard

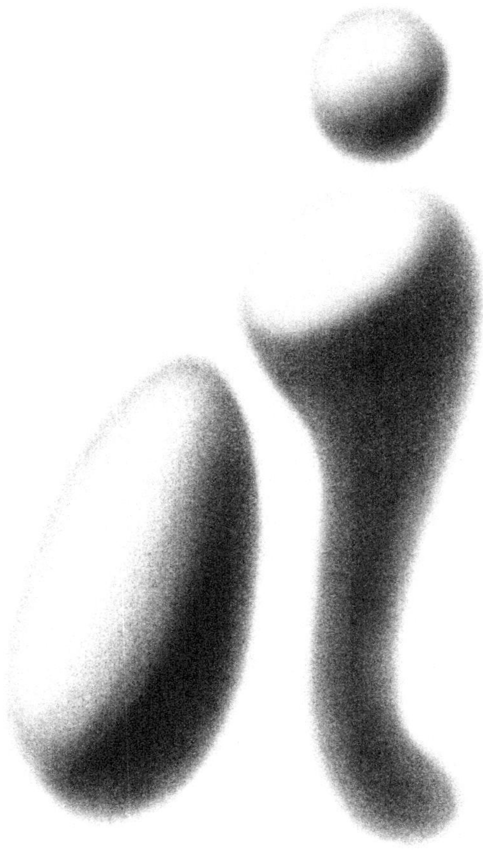

Till Then

I could be your companion till Mr. Right comes along
I can sing harmony if you invite me to sing on your song
How about a stroll down the beach without holding hands
We could be close without expectations or silly demands
We could ride out the storms and embrace the blue skies
It may appear I want you if you look deep into my eyes
People may think we're together, but we know that's not so
When Mr. Right arrives we'll simply let this friendship go
We're together even if I'm not yours and you're not mine
Till then let's laugh and enjoy life one moment at a time

り

Toes In The Water

Lying back on the sand with your toes in the water
The sky is aqua blue and the sun is getting hotter
It's only a lake, but to you it's your very own ocean
Distinctive summertime smells like coconut suntan lotion
Boats fly by and some have their radios up way too loud
You daydream peacefully over the sound of the crowd
The wind feels good and your troubles melt away
Life is tough, but you're not worrying about that today
The water is cold as goosebumps parade on your skin
Some days you feel like a loser, but today you will win
On the car ride home your lover gently touches your hair
Another memory stored, something later to share

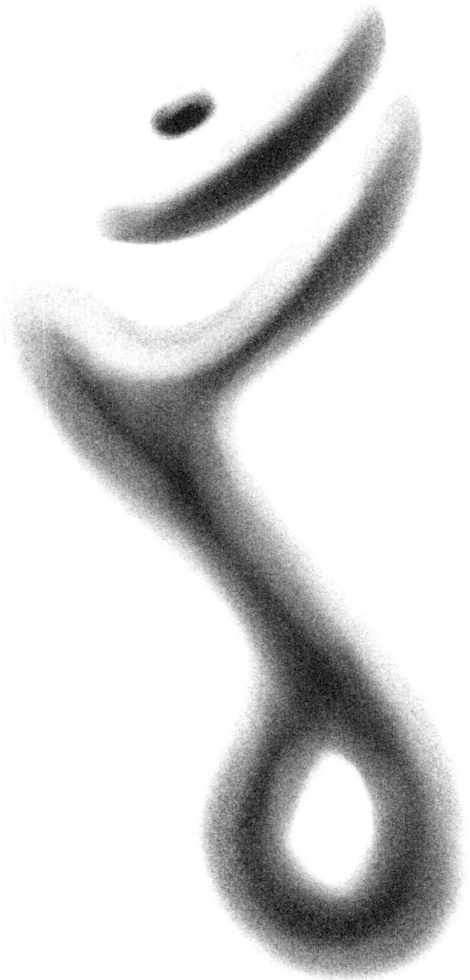

Trying

Chasing freedom only to be trapped in the end
They don't actually like you, they just like to pretend
The boss man waits as you punch in at the clock
How many windows can be broken with just one rock
The dreams are for sleeping and it's hard to fall asleep
Uphill battles on hills that are seemingly too steep
Fussing and fighting only to find out you were wrong
Summers are getting shorter while winters are getting long
Eagles fly high when they get a chance to leave the nest
Always keep trying, but chill out when you need to rest

ذ

Vantage Point

Senseless arguments then that slamming door sound
I have a little room to talk; I've been more than around
Mistakes by the thousands stacked neatly in my mind
What could I get myself into, and what trouble could I find
Was it youthful recklessness or was there a hurt inside
If you wanted to drive fast, I'd go along for the ride
Scars were cool, but now I don't think so anymore
A wild lion with a less than scary roar
Proving what I still haven't figured out
If I could do it over again, I'd pick a different route
The vantage point depths brought me back to the surface
I want to live a long happy life filled with love and purpose

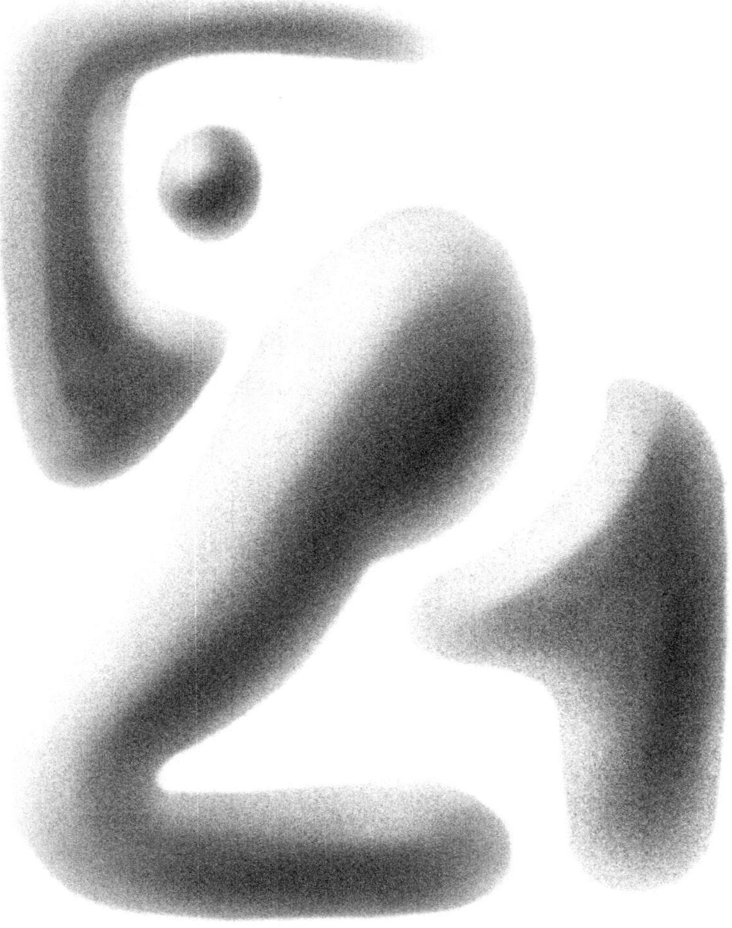

Wave

For some reason I feel the need to change for the better
Time to make myself accountable right down to the letter
One step forward without the two steps back
Lose the fear and work through the anxiety attack
Look compassionately for the beauty in each human being
Make it an award-winning movie, scene after scene
Pushing to accomplish so everyday brings forth meaning
Standing up straight when the world seems to be leaning
The words matter much less and the actions much more
No staring at the clock and no adding up the score
Flowing like a wave leaving the beach smooth and sandy
Never withholding love, instead giving it away like candy

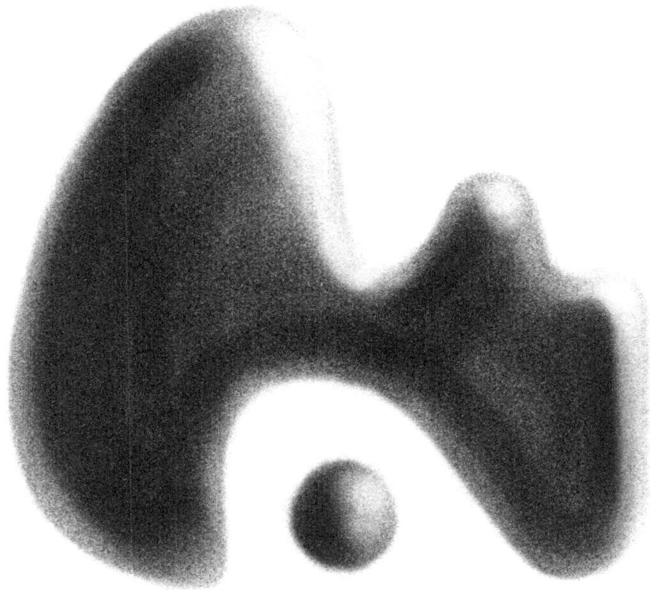

Wedding Girl

Those brown eyes and those seductive glances
Men flock nearer and are eager to take chances
I'm not that bold as my heart tends to beat faster
A small mishap on my part feels like such a disaster
Wine glass in her hand though she never takes a sip
She's overwhelmingly sexy when she bites her lower lip
So easy to photograph her in her natural light
She's all smiles while her eyes sparkle so bright
Her soft, beautiful hands have a vacancy for a ring
If I were a singer this would be the time to sing
The high heels removed and her hair now a new style
I should pack it in, but I think I'll hang out for a while
Spilled drinks, messy tables and a room way too hot
I should ask for her name, but maybe I better not

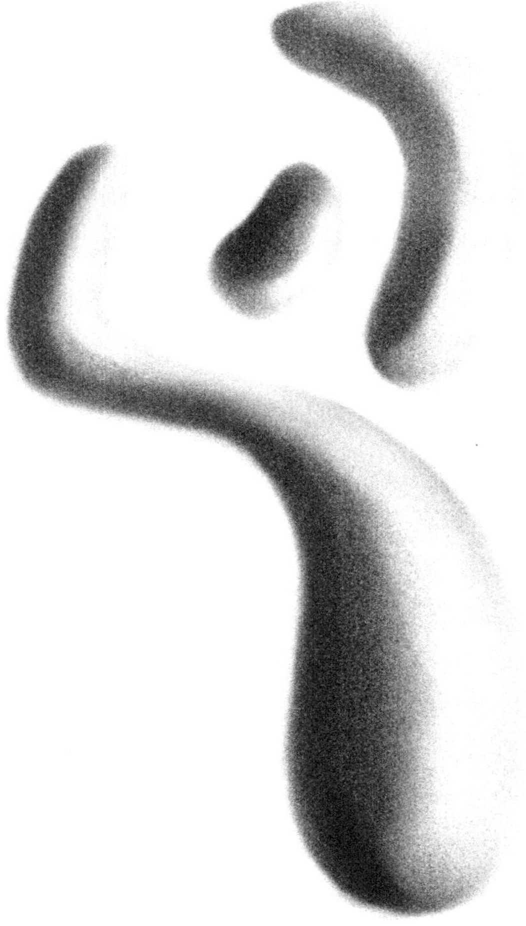

When Things Changed

That moment in time when everybody's life changed
Things suddenly stopped and needed to be rearranged
Simple things taken for granted became noticeably clear
A sunny day by the ocean with no one standing on the pier
The quiet streets and the sound of nothing being done
Minds like treadmills and other things that constantly run
Prayers sent up while the doors of the church are closed
Vulnerability in a situation where you might be exposed
A good time for brotherhood and a good time for reflection
Different skin tones yet together one beautiful complexion

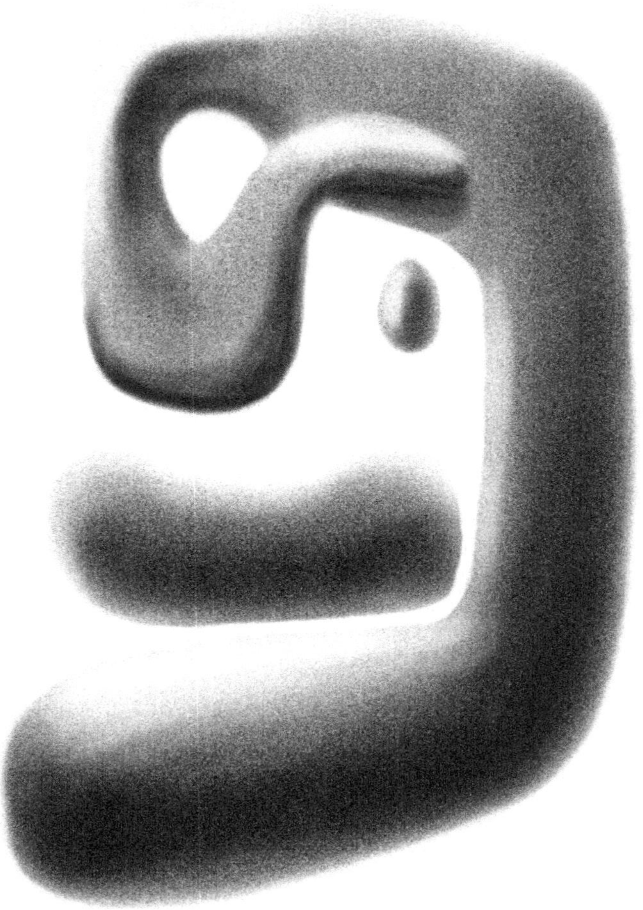

Yield

A box of broken crayons and a child creating art
Photographs taken to later develop on the heart
Cold emotions finding a wonderful reason to melt
When all the love in the world can finally be felt
Positive feelings driving away the depression
A beautiful smile leaving a lasting impression
Wrinkles artistically painted on a wise old face
Sitting by a lazy river and slowing down the pace
A ride in the country watching a tractor work the field
A need for nothing and a chance to finally yield

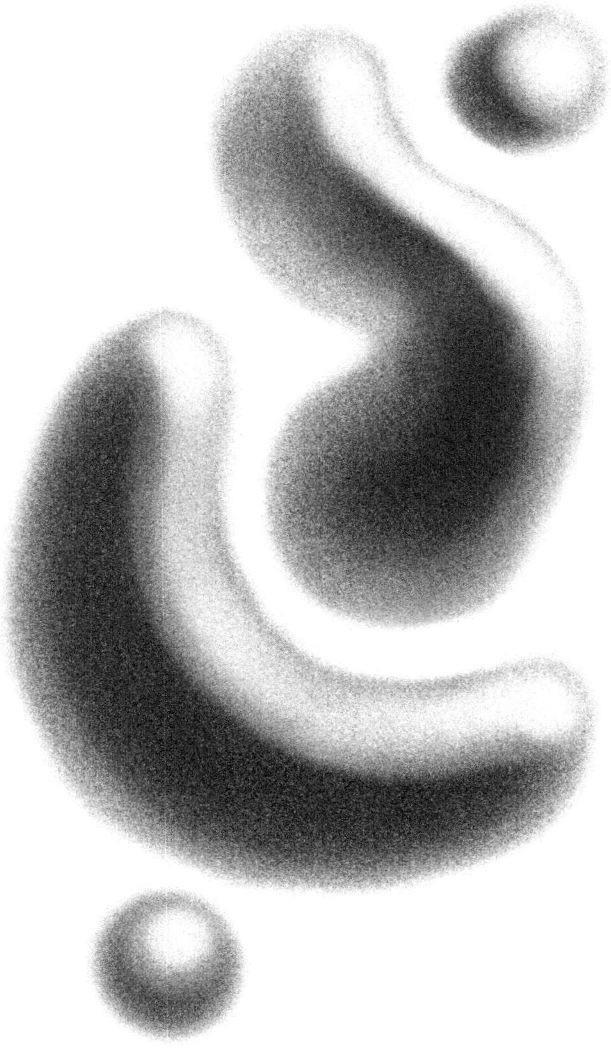

Made in the USA
Monee, IL
31 December 2020